ANIMALS UNDER THREAT

MOUNTAIN GORILLA

IN DANGER
EXTINCTION!

Marianne Taylor

Heinemann
LIBRARY

H **www.heinemann.co.uk/library**
Visit our website to find out more information about **Heinemann Library** books.

To order:
☎ Phone 44 (0) 1865 888066
▤ Send a fax to 44 (0) 1865 314091
▥ Visit the Heinemann Bookshop at www.heinemann.co.uk/library to browse our catalogue and order online.

First published in Great Britain by Heinemann Library, Halley Court, Jordan Hill, Oxford OX2 8EJ, part of Harcourt Education. Heinemann is a registered trademark of Harcourt Education Ltd.

Editorial: Emma Lynch, Jilly Attwood and Claire Throp
Design: Jo Hinton-Malivoire and Tokay, Bicester, UK (www.tokay.co.uk)
Picture Research: Rosie Garai and Liz Eddison
Production: Séverine Ribierre

Originated by Ambassador Litho Ltd
Printed in China by WKT Company Limited

ISBN 0 431 18890 4
08 07 06 05 04
10 9 8 7 6 5 4 3 2 1

British Library Cataloguing in Publication Data
Taylor, Marianne
Mountain gorilla - (Animals under threat)
599.8'84
A full catalogue record for this book is available from the British Library.

Acknowledgements
The Publishers would like to thank the following for permission to reproduce photographs: Ardea pp. **6**, **13** (Adrian Warren) **36** (D. Parer & E. Parer-Cook); Bruce Coleman p. **20** (Mary Plage); Corbis/Bettman p. **26**; Corbis/Gallo Images p. **10**, Gallo Images p. **21** (Martin Harvey); Corbis pp. **11** (Kennan Ward), **25** (Michael S. Lewis), **27** (Robert Maass), **29** (Yaan Arthus-Bertrand), **32** (Buddy Mays), **35** (Liba Taylor); Digital Vision pp. **4**, **5**, **7**, **17**, **34**, **40**; Ecoscene p. **23** (Karl Ammann); FLPA p. **12** (P Ward); Nature Picture Library p. **22** (Bruce Davidson); NHPA pp. **16**, **24**, **31** (Martin Harvey), **19** (Michael Leach); OSF pp. **8**, **38** (Andrew Plumptre); Rex p. **37** (Jeremy Williams); Rex/Sipa p. **28**; Steve Bloom pp. **14**, **18**, **30**; The Dian Fossey Gorilla Fund p. **42**; Tudor Photography p. **43**.

Cover photograph reproduced with permission of Corbis/Gallo Images/Martin Harvey.

The publishers would like to thank Dr Chris Tydeman, Environmental Consultant, for his assistance in the preparation of this book.

The author would like to thank A, A, J, M and T.

Disclaimer
All the Internet addresses (URLs) given in this book were valid at the time of going to press. However, due to the dynamic nature of the Internet, some addresses may have changed, or sites may have ceased to exist since publication. While the author and publishers regret any inconvenience this may cause readers, no responsibility for any such changes can be accepted by either the author or the publishers.

Every effort has been made to contact copyright holders of any material reproduced in this book. Any omissions will be rectified in subsequent printings if notice is given to the publishers.

The paper used to print this book comes from sustainable resources.

Contents

Words printed in the text in bold, **like this**, are explained in the Glossary.

The mountain gorilla

The mountain gorilla is the ultimate **great ape**. It is famous for its huge size and tremendous strength, but it is a peaceful, gentle animal. Mountain gorillas live quietly in the remote mountain forests of central Africa. They are the best known, but also the rarest, kind of gorilla. There are so few of them left that they are in real danger of becoming **extinct** if they are not protected from the many threats they face.

Gorillas are the largest type of **ape** in the world. The other great apes are orang-utans, chimpanzees, bonobos and humans. The much smaller gibbons and siamangs are also apes. Apes belong to the group of **mammals** called **primates**. Monkeys, lemurs and bushbabies are also primates. Of all the animals in the world, gorillas are one of the closest living relatives to humans. Ninety-eight per cent of the gorilla's **genes** are the same as ours. All the large apes are rare and threatened with extinction, except for humans. We are the most common large mammals in the world, but our success has often been at the expense of other animals.

gorilla   chimpanzee   orang-utan   gibbon

▲ *The great apes are the largest primates. They are all big, powerful animals, with large heads and no tails. The gibbon is a smaller type of ape.*

History and discovery of mountain gorillas

It is thought that many thousands of years ago, all gorillas in Africa were alike. However, as the forest they lived in became smaller and more broken up over the centuries, the gorilla population was split into three groups. The longer the three separate populations of gorillas were isolated from each other, the more different they became.

In 1902, a German explorer called Captain von Beringe became the first European to see mountain gorillas. He was exploring what is now the country Rwanda, in central Africa. Halfway up Mount Sabyinyo in the Virungas range, Beringe saw what he described as a 'herd of big, black monkeys' climbing a hillside. His men shot and killed two of them. Beringe could not identify the animals, which were so much bigger than the gorillas of the lowlands. He brought one of them back to the natural history museum in Berlin, where it was recognized as a new gorilla **subspecies**. The mountain gorilla, as it became known, was given the scientific name *Gorilla gorilla beringei*, in honour of Beringe.

The mountain gorilla is the largest, most powerful primate in the world.

How many species of gorilla?

Until recently, there was thought to be only one **species** of gorilla, divided into three subspecies. These were the eastern lowland gorilla, western lowland gorilla and mountain gorilla. However, at the end of the 20th century new scientific methods of **genetic testing** were used to study these three kinds of gorilla. The results have suggested that the western lowland gorilla is probably genetically different enough from the other two to be treated as a separate species, which could not breed with the other two.

Gorilla country

Mountain gorillas live in forests on the slopes of several extinct volcanoes called the Virunga mountain range. They are also found in a forest 20 miles north of the Virungas, called the Bwindi Impenetrable Forest, in Uganda. The total area crosses the borders of three African countries: Rwanda, Uganda and the Democratic Republic of the Congo (DRC) (see map on page 9). At their highest points these mountains are extremely cold, with very few plants, but lower down the slopes there are various types of forest. The gorillas are found in the **montane**, **cloud-forest** zone, at 3000–3500 metres above sea level. Here, the jungle is dense, with lush vegetation. However, this is not a tropical forest: the temperature ranges from 7 to 20 °C, and it often rains and hails.

▲ *Although the forests lie close to the **equator**, they are so high up the mountain-side that they are always cold and misty.*

A variety of wildlife

Gorilla habitat is good for all sorts of wildlife. The cloud-forest is rich with a variety of plants that in turn support many **species** of animal. The gorillas share the forest with buffaloes, forest elephants, leopards, several kinds of antelope and chimpanzees. The forest also has several kinds of monkey and other smaller **mammals**, and around 300 species of bird.

The forest vegetation is very lush, so mountain gorillas can find plenty of plants to eat.

Forest food

Mountain gorillas are mainly **herbivores**. There is plenty of food for them in the forest, but some of the plants they feed on grow very slowly. After eating all the best bits of vegetation in one place, a gorilla group will move to a new area of forest, so that the vegetation has a chance to grow back. They therefore need to live in a much larger area of forest than they will actually be using at any one time.

One favourite food is bamboo shoots, which grow during the wettest times of year. So the gorillas spend more time in the bamboo forest areas during the rainy seasons. Occasionally they go higher up, into the subalpine meadows (4000 metres above sea level) where temperatures are below freezing at night and there is less suitable food for them. However, the giant senecio tree is found here, and the soft centre of its twigs is one of the mountain gorilla's favourite foods.

Habitat change

African forests are much smaller and more broken up than they were many years ago. Most of central Africa was covered in rainforest 5000–7000 years ago, and there were probably many more gorillas then. The climate has gradually become drier, causing some of the forests to be replaced by other kinds of vegetation. In the last century, people have cleared vast areas of the remaining forest, to use the wood and to create new farmland. Now, the area of suitable mountain gorilla **habitat** that remains is so small, it cannot support many gorillas.

Gorilla populations

The mountain gorillas' two areas of **habitat** are small and isolated, and they do not venture away from them. Researchers have carefully and thoroughly studied both areas for many years, and the gorilla population has been monitored very closely. A great deal is known about the way gorillas use their habitat, and about how much space each group needs. Also, there is so much research going on that many of the groups are seen and counted quite regularly. This means that the estimates of the total population are probably quite accurate. The most recent surveys of mountain gorilla numbers suggest that the total population is about 670.

The total population is divided into two main groups. About 355 mountain gorillas live in the Virunga range. The area they live in falls in three countries, each of which protects its gorilla area as a **national park**. The countries (and their national parks) are Rwanda (Parc National des Volcans), Uganda (Mgahinga Gorilla National Park), and the DRC (Virunga National Park). A separate population of about 292 is found in southwest Uganda, about 20 miles north of the Virungas, in the Bwindi National Park. Some scientists believe that the gorillas found here are a distinct **subspecies** called the Bwindi Gorilla, *Gorilla gorilla bwindi*.

Gorillas always stay within the forest areas, and will not cross into the farmland that comes right to the forest edge.

The mountain gorilla is found in two tiny areas of forest in central Africa.

Close to the edge

At the beginning of the 1980s, **extinction** seemed inevitable for the mountain gorilla. There were only 250 in existence. Extremely dedicated and determined **conservationists** have worked hard to protect them since then. As a result of their efforts, the number of mountain gorillas has slowly increased over the past 20 years. Nevertheless, it is still a critically **endangered** animal.

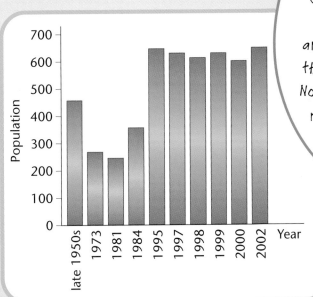

Map labels

Bwindi National Park

Uganda

DRC (formerly known as Zaire)

Mgahinga Gorilla National Park

Virunga National Park

Parc National des Volcans

Rwanda

Lake Kivu

So few gorillas, so many people

Without very strict and careful conservation, we could lose one of our closest relatives from the world for good. Mountain gorillas have never lived anywhere other than central Africa, and they may never have been very common. Now they are extremely rare. For every mountain gorilla in the world there are more than nine million human beings.

Chart

Population vs Year

Year	Population
late 1950s	~460
1973	~270
1981	~245
1984	~360
1995	~650
1997	~635
1998	~615
1999	~635
2000	~605
2002	~655

This chart shows how the population of mountain gorillas has changed over the past 50 years.

The body of a gorilla

Mountain gorillas are powerfully built animals, with broad shoulders, long, muscular arms and short, sturdy legs. They have strong, compact bodies with big, round bellies. Their necks are short and thick, and they have big heads with strong jaws and thick skulls. Their great size and bulk means that very few animals ever hunt and kill them. Having a big, chunky body also helps them to keep warm – the mountain forests they live in become extremely cold at night.

Males and females

Male mountain gorillas can weigh up to 200 kilograms, and average 160 kilograms. They can be up to 1.8 metres tall when they stand up. Females are much smaller, weighing 70–114 kilograms, and are rarely more than 1.2 metres tall. As well as being bigger than females, males have large, sharp **canine** teeth. These big teeth are not for eating or hunting, but are used in **displays** of strength and **aggression** between male gorillas. Usually, just the sight of a big male gorilla standing up and baring his huge teeth, while loudly slapping his massive chest, is enough to put off any other gorilla from attacking him. Actual fighting is rare, but if they have to, they will use their teeth and can inflict a very severe bite.

▲ *An adult male gorilla shows his huge canine teeth.*

Mountain gorillas are long-lived animals: their natural lifespan is probably 40–50 years. However, only about half of them survive to be adults. Once they are adult, the natural dangers they face, like disease or accidental injury, are not nearly as serious as the dangers posed by the activities of humans.

Wrapped up warm

The fur of a mountain gorilla is long, thick and silky, and usually dark brown to blackish-grey. It covers most of the gorilla's body, except for the middle of the face, palms of the hands and soles of the feet. Their fur is much longer than that of lowland gorillas, which do not have to cope with such low temperatures. The hair on the backs of males becomes silvery-white as they grow older. Adult male gorillas are called **silverbacks**.

Getting about

Young mountain gorillas enjoy climbing and playing in the trees, but adults prefer to stay on the ground. They can climb if they need to, as long as they stick to branches sturdy enough to bear their weight. However, there is plenty of food close to the ground, so this is where they spend most of their time. They can stand up on two legs, and even walk like this for short periods, but their long arms and short legs mean that they prefer to move about on all fours, walking on their feet and hands.

When gorillas walk on all fours they curl their hands into fists, so they are actually walking on their knuckles. They leave four knuckle prints in the ground.

Gorilla lifestyle

The mountain gorilla's usual lifestyle is rather a pleasant one. They are sociable animals, spending most of their lives as a member of a fairly stable group, and there is usually very little conflict among the members of the group. The forest has plenty of the plants they like to eat, and they have little need to worry about being attacked by other animals. A **silverback** gorilla will fearlessly defend his group if danger threatens, but no natural **predator** would try to take on a huge adult male mountain gorilla. So gorilla groups are usually left undisturbed.

Gorillas are not very lively. They spend most of their time resting. Only the young gorillas play energetically together; the adults prefer to laze around, sleeping, feeding, digesting their last meal and grooming each other. They usually feed for several hours in the morning and again in the afternoon, and take a long nap in the middle of the day. They regularly travel around the forest to find new feeding grounds, but they move at a leisurely pace, travelling less than half a kilometre per day. These animals are very laid-back indeed.

Young gorillas are livelier and more adventurous than adults.

Mountain gorillas are well protected from the cold and rain of the forest by their long hair.

Sleeping arrangements

Gorillas are diurnal, which means they are awake during the day and sleep at night. Each night they build simple nests to sleep in. Sleeping in a nest helps to keep out the chill of the night. The nests are made out of vegetation, and may be built in tree branches or on the ground. Small babies share a nest with their mothers, but otherwise each adult and **weaned juvenile** builds its own nest. Gorillas learn how to construct a nest at an early age, and become very efficient at it. Usually, the nest-building takes only a few minutes.

What's on the menu?

The gorillas' food supply is all around them, so they rarely climb trees to **forage**, although they are capable climbers in trees that can bear their weight. Their big bellies contain long digestive systems to cope with their vegetable diet, which consists mostly of the roots, leaves, stems and pith of plants. Their large intestines are roughly twice the size of ours. A male adult gorilla eats up to 30 kilograms of vegetation in a day. They occasionally eat **invertebrates**, such as beetle larvae and ants but, unlike the closely-related chimpanzee, they never hunt other **mammals**.

Hair care

Gorillas are very clean animals, and spend time every day grooming their fur. They also groom each other's fur, removing any skin **parasites** they find. This mutual grooming is a good way to keep the fur in good condition, and to enjoy a good scratch of those hard-to-reach places. It is also a form of close, trusting contact, which helps to establish and maintain friendships between individuals.

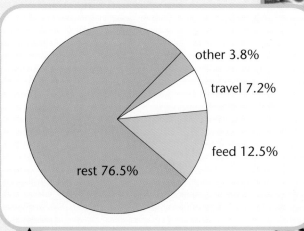

other 3.8%

travel 7.2%

feed 12.5%

rest 76.5%

This pie-chart shows how mountain gorillas spend their time.

Gorilla groups

Most mountain gorilla groups have only one adult male or **silverback**, sometimes known as the **alpha male**, and two or more adult females. The rest of the group consists of their offspring, babies and **juveniles** of various ages and both sexes. The alpha male is the dominant member of the group. He decides what the group does and where it goes. He is bigger and stronger than all the others, so they very rarely try to fight him. He is usually the father of all the young gorillas in the group. Among the adult females, the one who was first to join the group will usually be dominant over the one who arrived next, and so on, although when females have babies their rank may improve.

The usual group size is around 7–14 animals. Sometimes much larger groups form, with 30 or more members. Big groups might include two or more silverbacks, because one silverback on his own cannot be in

A typical mountain gorilla group, with one adult male, several adult females and several juveniles of both sexes.

charge of so many gorillas. However, where there are two or more silverbacks, one is dominant over the others. Larger groups seem to be less stable, often breaking up into smaller groups.

When it's time to leave the group

Males leave the group they were born into when they are around eleven years old. They then live alone, because they cannot join an established group – the alpha male will drive them away. They must wait until they find their first female and can start a new group. They usually do not start a group until they are at least fifteen, so they spend at least four years living alone. Ten per cent of the total mountain gorilla population is made up of solitary males, who have not yet acquired a **harem**, or group of females.

Females leave the group they were born into and move straight to a new group when they are around eight years old. They then begin to breed. They may join a lone male and start a new group. Females often choose to do this, rather than join an established group and be a lower-ranking female.

The young challengers

Sometimes one solitary young male will try to take over an established group. The alpha male of that group will usually be able to drive him away with **aggressive** displays. However, if they are closely matched in strength they may fight fiercely. If the newcomer defeats the alpha male and takes over the group, he will often then attack and kill all the young gorillas in the group. This is thought to be so that the females will become ready to breed again more quickly. The new male will not have to spend time looking after the old male's offspring, but will start fathering babies of his own so he can pass on his **genes**.

As they spend almost all of their lives as members of a group, it is important for gorillas to get along with each other. There is very little conflict within a group, because they do not normally have to compete with each other for food, mating opportunities or other resources. The **silverback** is in overall charge of the group, followed by the most dominant adult female, and then the other adult females. The larger **juveniles** are dominant over smaller, younger ones. If any fights threaten to break out among the females or juveniles, the silverback will end the dispute with displays of **aggression** towards those involved.

Gorilla voices

Gorillas are far quieter than their cousins the chimpanzees, who make shrill, shrieking cries. However, they do communicate with sound. Their voices are low-pitched and the sounds they make are usually quite soft, perhaps because they are rarely more than a few metres away from each other. Researchers have so far identified around 20 different sounds that gorillas make with their voices, a variety of grunts, howls, hoots and barks. Gorillas also beat their chests or the ground with cupped hands. Chest beating is a display of dominance, most often performed by the **alpha male**.

Dominant gorillas often get groomed by those of a lower rank.

No territories, large home ranges

Gorilla groups do not have **territories**. This means that they do not live in one specific area, which they defend from other gorillas, but move about freely within the entire forest. To allow the vegetation they eat to regrow, groups must travel to new feeding grounds regularly. Although they move around a lot, they do not wander at random but stay within a particular large area, or home range, which is usually several square kilometres. They sometimes encounter other groups or solitary males on their travels. When this happens the males will show aggression by chest beating, growling and teeth baring, and they may even physically fight.

How clever are gorillas?

Like other **apes**, gorillas are very intelligent animals. In studies, captive western lowland gorillas have been taught sign language, and they have used the signs to form simple sentences. They are able to ask for food or drink, and describe objects in terms of their size and colour. It is thought that they can also express abstract ideas, for example, they will 'talk' about objects that are not with them at the time. We do not know whether wild gorillas use anything that could be described as a language. For all the years of study, we cannot yet 'speak gorilla' and understand fully what they 'say' to each other with their sounds and gestures. But the sign language studies suggest that they may well be able to communicate with each other at a quite complex level.

Play is an important way of learning social behaviours.

Courtship and breeding

A female gorilla starts **breeding** when she is about eight to ten years old. Males are usually in their mid-teens before they have attracted the first female of their group and have their first opportunity to breed.

This male and female are courting.

Courtship

For a few days in each month, a female gorilla goes into oestrus, which means she is ready to mate and become pregnant. At this time, she will approach the **silverback** of her group. She stares at him with her lips pursed, and may follow him around or reach out to him. After she has gained his attention in this way, the two will mate. The silverback mates with all the females in his group when they go into oestrus. Because their groups are very stable and usually have only one adult male, gorilla courtship is quite simple. In some other **primates**, like chimpanzees, the breeding system is quite different. Females choose mates from several available males, so males have to compete with each other to impress the females, making courtship a more important part of their lives.

Pregnancy and birth

A female gorilla's pregnancy lasts eight and a half months, after which a single baby is born, or occasionally twins. It usually only takes a few minutes for the baby to be born. The mother usually will not become pregnant again until her baby is about four years old, so she has a long time to devote to the care of each baby. This is important, because baby gorillas grow slowly and have a lot to learn from their mothers. Usually, gorillas are devoted mothers who take great care of their babies.

Gorilla mothers have a baby once every four or five years.

Gorillas and women

A lot of old legends about gorillas, both in Africa and elsewhere, suggest that male gorillas will grab human females if they get a chance. In some African cultures, women will not go on their own to areas where gorillas are found, in case they are chased by a lovelorn silverback. In the famous film *King Kong*, the giant gorilla King Kong falls in love with a human female. He seizes her and runs away with her. In truth, an adult silverback will have a **harem** of several female gorillas, all of whom seem more interested in him than he is in them!

Young gorillas

A newborn mountain gorilla baby is completely dependent on its mother, for her milk and her protection from danger. She keeps the baby close to her at all times, holding it against her chest. A baby gorilla has stronger hands, arms and legs than a human baby, so it can cling quite tightly to its mother's body and will not fall off if she needs to use both hands to climb, provided she moves carefully.

Caring for the baby

New mother gorillas will know a bit about caring for a baby from watching other females. However, first babies often do not survive, sometimes because of the mother's lack of experience. She has to learn to keep her baby very close and not to leave it on its own, when **predators** might take it. She must also be careful not to let the other gorillas too close while it is still very small. Sometimes, other members of the group will injure or kill a baby gorilla in their eagerness to play with it. As mothers gain experience, the survival rate of their babies improves.

Baby gorillas are very appealing. Unfortunately this makes them targets for poachers, who try to capture and sell them.

Baby snatchers

Baby gorillas are lively bundles of black fluff. They have round faces and wide eyes, without the 'frowning' expression of adult gorillas. Their charming appearance and delightful character make them desirable animals for people who keep zoos. They are also much easier to handle than fully grown gorillas, which can overpower people. Animal traders will pay a lot of money for gorilla babies, so **poachers** often try to capture them to sell to traders.

The early years

A very young baby clings to its mother's chest all the time. After a few months it will begin to ride on her back. By the time it is a year old, the baby is beginning to eat solid plant food. However, it carries on taking milk from its mother until it is about three years old. The baby slowly learns from its mother and the other gorillas in the group which foods are best and how to find them.

Becoming independent

As they grow bigger and stronger, young gorillas spend more time away from their mothers and begin to play with other youngsters in the trees. By the time they are five, they can **forage** perfectly well by themselves, and their mothers will usually be caring for the next new baby. The young gorillas spend about three more years with the group they were born in, growing bigger and stronger and learning about the forest and how to be a gorilla. They learn a great deal through play. When they eventually leave to join another group or start a new group, they have all the skills they need to survive as adults.

▲ Up here, a baby gorilla is safe from danger and gets a good view of their world.

Conflict between gorillas and humans

Long ago, mountain gorillas had very little to fear from other animals. The only large **predator** that shares their **habitat** is the leopard, but even this famously brave and strong big cat would not take on a **silverback** gorilla defending his group. There have been a few cases of leopards attacking lone female or **juvenile** mountain gorillas, but this is very unusual. But human beings with guns or spears can kill adult mountain gorillas, and they have been doing so for many years.

Hunting for meat

Mountain gorillas have been hunted for meat for many years, but not often. Many populations of wild animals are not harmed by small-scale hunting, but there are so few mountain gorillas that even occasional hunting is a serious problem. For the local people eating gorilla meat is **taboo**, but in desperate times that taboo will be broken. Gorillas can also be accidentally caught in **snares** set by hunters to catch other animals, like antelope.

▲ *Some people have always found the idea of hunting big, powerful animals exciting, although this attitude is far less common now than it was a hundred years ago.*

Poaching

In more recent times, gorillas have been hunted for other reasons besides food. There are people who sell or collect items made from the body parts of wild animals, including gorillas. Unbelievably, a bin made from an elephant's foot, or an ashtray made from a dead gorilla's hand, are considered attractive and valuable trophies by some people. There is a market for gorilla heads, feet and hands. The rarity and size of mountain gorillas mean that their body parts are especially valuable, so prices for them are very high. This kind of hunting is often called **poaching**. The fact that the gorillas' habitat is protected, and that killing them is illegal, is not always enough to put off the poachers, because they can make a lot of money this way.

Taken alive

There are also people willing to pay thousands, or even hundreds of thousands of pounds for living mountain gorillas, to keep in zoos and private animal collections. To satisfy this demand, poachers try to catch baby gorillas alive. But gorilla mothers keep their babies close to them, and all the gorillas will fight fiercely if their group is attacked. Therefore the hunters will usually have to kill some adult gorillas in order to capture a baby.

Killed for the cure?

Many kinds of animal are killed by poachers, and their body parts sold to make traditional medicines. The larger, rarer and more spectacular the animal, the more it is sought after. In traditional medicine, powdered tiger bone is believed to cure many illnesses. Some African cultures use medicines derived from gorillas.

Workers will attempt to return this rescued baby to the wild.

Destroying gorilla habitats

As people have increased in number, developed more sophisticated tools and spread throughout the world, they have made great changes to most types of natural **habitat**.

The gorillas' habitat is totally destroyed by forest clearance.

Woodland is of little use to people as a habitat to live in or cultivate, but the trees supply wood, which is extremely useful. As the trees are felled, the cleared land can be used for farming or other kinds of **development**. The wood from some of the trees that grow in the Virungas is quite valuable, and some of it is sold to other countries. It is also used locally as firewood. **Logging** has recently taken place in the mountain gorilla forests, although they are supposed to be protected. In 1969, almost half the area of the Parc National des Volcans was felled to create new farmland.

Slow to grow

Ancient forest takes a huge amount of time to regrow. The biggest trees may be several hundred years old. Forests planted by people for wood production tend to contain fast-growing tree **species**, which are ready to be felled in just a few decades. They support far fewer animals than the rich, varied natural forests. It is not possible to replace quickly the habitat that the gorillas have lost.

The need for farmland

The human population of the countries where mountain gorillas live is growing all the time. These people need to eat, and so they need land on which to plant crops and graze their domestic animals. The governments of the countries want to protect their unique wildlife, but they also have a duty to help people develop productive farmland. The pressure on what remains of the **cloud-forest** is tremendous. To the desperately hungry people, the forest may look like wasted land that could be being used to grow food. In 1983, the government of Rwanda seriously considered allowing a further 12,000 acres of the Parc National des Volcans to be cleared for agriculture. Meanwhile, local people enter the forest and cut firewood or graze their **livestock** there. So the forest is continually being eaten away.

As their habitat shrinks, the gorillas are beginning to find it more difficult to find food. There are a few reports of gorillas **foraging** among pea and maize fields in farmland. This creates yet more conflict between the gorillas and the local people.

These terraces make it possible to farm on very steep slopes. This can lead to encroachment onto gorilla territory.

Saving gorilla habitats

Carl Akeley was a gorilla hunter who became a campaigner for their conservation.

It was the explorer Carl Akeley who first strongly campaigned for the **conservation** of mountain gorillas and their **habitat**. In 1921 he went on a mission to the Virunga Mountains, to take mountain gorilla specimens for the American Museum of Natural History. He and his party killed several gorillas, but on examining a dead **silverback** Akeley had a sudden change of heart. He was struck by the gorillas' humanlike appearance, and he began to feel that it was wrong to kill animals that were so like ourselves. He had also come to realize how rare the animals were. He approached the Belgian government, which controlled that area of Africa at the time, and suggested that the mountain gorillas should not be killed, but protected.

National parks

Due to the efforts of Akeley and others, the Albert National Park was established by the Belgian government on 21 April 1925, to protect its mountain gorillas. It was the first **national park** to be established in Africa. On 9 July 1929, the boundaries of the park were extended to include almost the entire Virunga volcano chain. The area remains officially protected land, even though the boundaries and administration of the countries it falls in have changed several times. Today Rwanda, Uganda and the **DRC** each protect their own area of Virungas forest as a national park, but the forest is continuous across the three countries. It is an island of wild habitat in the middle of densely populated, farmed land.

The other, separate mountain gorilla area, Bwindi Impenetrable Forest in Uganda, became a Forest Reserve in 1932. Its trees were protected and any tree felling was strictly controlled. At this time, the protected area was at the centre of a much larger area of unprotected forest. By the end of the 1980s, the unprotected forest areas had all been felled. The remaining area, the Forest Reserve, was declared a national park in 1991. Study of the gorillas in Bwindi National Park has been going on ever since.

George Schaller

Biologist George Schaller came to the park in 1959 to carry out the first serious, thorough field study of mountain gorillas. Assisted by his wife Kay, he spent a year working with the gorillas. The animals became **habituated** to them and after a while accepted their close presence. George Schaller was able to record details of mountain gorilla behaviour that had never been seen before. He subsequently wrote a book, *The Year of the Gorilla*, which is still extremely useful for researchers studying these animals. The knowledge the Schallers gained about the gorilla population and way of life has since helped conservationists decide how best to protect the animals and their habitat.

George Schaller carried out the first detailed study of mountain gorilla behaviour.

Dian Fossey

Dian Fossey was the most famous mountain gorilla researcher. She was born in California in 1932, and grew up with a great love of animals and wildlife. She saw her first mountain gorillas during a holiday in Zaire (the country now known as the **DRC**) in 1963. She was enthralled by the magnificent animals.

Appendicitis?

The anthropologist Dr Louis Leakey met Fossey on her first trip to Zaire. In 1967 he met her again in London, and asked her if she would like to work for him studying mountain gorillas. Fossey jumped at the chance. Leakey said she would have to have her appendix removed before she could return to Zaire, because the operation could not be carried out there if she happened to need it. She had the operation, but then discovered that it was not necessary at all – Leakey was just testing her determination to work with the gorillas!

Getting closer

Fossey began studying gorillas in Zaire in 1966. After a few months she moved to Parc National des Volcans in Rwanda, where she established a new camp called Karisoke. She spent many years at this camp, studying the gorillas. By quietly imitating their behaviour, she managed to gain their trust and could soon sit close to them without alarming them. In 1970 she became the first person to have 'friendly contact' with a wild mountain gorilla when a young male called Peanuts approached her and touched her hand.

Dian Fossey gradually earned the trust of wild mountain gorillas.

Fossey spent much of her life working with her team at her camp, Karisoke. Here, she shows the poachers' snares found in the forest.

The gorillas' champion

Fossey was a tireless campaigner for gorilla **conservation**. She introduced extra patrols of guards and instructed them to capture any **poachers** they found. She also worked to prevent cattle grazing inside the park, and fiercely resisted the attempts of the Rwandan government to allow gorilla tourism.

In 1978, poachers killed her favourite gorilla, a **silverback** known as Digit. Fossey was grief-stricken, and became even more determined to protect the gorillas she considered to be her friends. Some said that she became dangerously obsessed with finding and punishing poachers. She eventually made many enemies in Rwanda through her determined and uncompromising views. One of these enemies turned out to be deadly – on 26 December 1985, Dian Fossey was found murdered in her cabin. To this day, it is not known who killed her.

A lasting legacy

Fossey's contribution to mountain gorilla conservation was huge. The Digit Fund, started by Fossey in 1978, is now known as The Dian Fossey Gorilla Fund International. It continues to raise money, fund research and run the Karisoke Research Centre. Other similar organizations have since been established, such as The Mountain Gorilla Fund. Fossey's book *Gorillas in the Mist*, and the film based on it, have done much to raise public awareness of the plight of mountain gorillas.

Gorilla tourism

The mountain gorillas of the Virungas were, by the 1980s, one of the best-known populations of large wild **mammals** in the world. The problems of **habitat**-loss, hunting and **poaching** were also well understood. It was clear that the gorillas were very seriously threatened with **extinction**. It was therefore essential to protect them and their habitat. The cost of providing this protection is huge, so new ways to make money were needed.

Ecotourism means small-scale tourism, which involves local people, has a low impact on the environment and uses the money raised to help fund **conservation**. In the 1980s the Rwandan government began to organize gorilla-watching tours to raise money. The idea was not supported by everyone involved in gorilla conservation, but it quickly became a very useful source of income for the country. As well as helping to fund the protection of the park, ecotourism made the gorillas more valuable to Rwanda in their own right, as living animals. The other gorilla parks also began to host gorilla tours.

▲ *Watched by local children, gorilla-watchers set off for the forest at the Parc des Virunga, DRC.*

Fame and fortune

Far from Africa, mountain gorillas were becoming stars of the screen. In 1988 the film *Gorillas in the Mist*, about the life of Dian Fossey, was released and became a box-office hit. People in the UK had already seen mountain gorillas on television, in the ground-breaking natural history series *Life on Earth* (first screened in 1979). British natural history broadcaster David Attenborough sat among a group of mountain gorillas. The animals played gently with him, completely relaxed in his presence. All this led to an increase in tourism, as people wanted to go out and see these wonderful creatures for themselves.

Is it harmful?

Some researchers are concerned that gorilla tourism may not always be good for the animals. It is certainly a good way of making money, but the welfare of the gorillas must come first. Some tours get too close to gorillas, or bring groups of 30 or more tourists. Tourism has quickly grown in popularity, but the research into its effects on gorillas has not kept up. Some scientists say that gorilla tourism should be more strictly controlled than it is at present.

Tourists who are lucky enough to see these animals in the wild are unlikely to forget the experience.

Visiting the relatives

In the Virungas, ten **habituated** gorilla groups are used for tourist visits. Tourists, in groups of six to eight, can watch the gorillas from as close as 5 metres, for up to an hour. The park guards are with them at all times, making sure they do not get too close to the gorillas or disturb them in any way. Tourists who have been on these tours describe the experience as quite magical.

Gorillas in contact with humans

If it had not been possible for researchers like Dian Fossey to **habituate** mountain gorillas to the close presence of humans, our knowledge of their way of life would be much less complete. There would also be very little chance of creating a successful **ecotourism** industry based around seeing mountain gorillas. However, this habituation comes at a price.

Captive lowland gorillas, like this one, are gentle with their keepers and any 'accidental visitors'.

Infectious diseases

Gorillas could catch many of the diseases that affect humans. However, the outbreak of an **infectious disease** could be much worse for them, because they have no natural **immunity** to it, never having been exposed to it before. There are cases of captive lowland gorillas catching measles from humans. The wild population of mountain gorillas is so small that any infectious disease could be disastrous for them. If a tourist has an illness, they are not allowed to approach the gorillas. Thanks to these measures, there have so far been no known cases of an illness being passed from humans to gorillas.

Too close for comfort?

Another possible problem with habituation is that the gorillas could become too trusting of humans, and lose their natural wariness around us. This could increase the risk of groups being attacked by **poachers**. It is also possible that the close human contact is stressful and harmful to the gorillas in subtle ways. One well-watched group in the Bwindi National Park lost seven of its original ten members at the end of the 1990s, and no-one is sure why this happened.

There is also the potential risk of the gorillas harming their human visitors. Gorillas are certainly powerful enough to harm or injure humans. There are no recorded fatal attacks, but some researchers have been on the receiving end of **aggressive** displays from **silverbacks**, and once or twice a researcher has been charged at and knocked down. It is important never to surprise the gorillas, block their path, reach for them or do anything that might seem threatening to them. Respectful and intelligent behaviour from visitors and researchers is necessary at all times.

Peaceful gorillas

When they do not feel threatened, gorillas pose no danger to humans. The rewarding experiences of Dian Fossey and many others who have spent time with mountain gorilla groups reveal how gentle they really are. This seems to be true of all kinds of gorilla, not just the habituated mountain gorillas of the Virungas. On two occasions children have fallen into lowland gorilla enclosures at zoos, injuring themselves in the process. Onlookers were horrified and expected the worst, but in both cases the gorillas treated the injured children with great care and gentleness, 'standing guard' over them until they were taken away by keepers.

The countries in which mountain gorillas live have long histories of conflict. There is an ongoing struggle between two tribes, the Hutus and the Tutsis, for control of the area. This conflict recently erupted into one of the most terrible wars of the last century. The war began in 1990, when rebel forces invaded Rwanda from neighbouring Uganda, intending to overthrow the Rwandan government. Although another four years were to pass before the war reached its height, the effect of the invasion on Rwanda's tourism industry was immediate. No-one wanted to risk being caught up in a war, for the sake of seeing mountain gorillas.

Several gorillas were killed by soldiers during the war, including silverbacks trying to defend their groups.

In the firing line

Hundreds of thousands of people died in the war. It was not surprising that the researchers and park keepers could do little to keep the mountain gorillas safe in the midst of such a large-scale human tragedy. A popular **habituated silverback** known as Mrithi was an early gorilla casualty. On 21 May 1992, soldiers shot and killed him after surprising him and his group. Although the rest of the group escaped, their future social structure was bound to be disrupted by the loss of their leader. Up to fourteen more gorillas have been killed during the war, many by **poachers** taking full advantage of the disruption. The situation was too dangerous for any gorilla workers to remain in the area. In 1994 the camp at Karisoke was closed.

*The gorillas' **habitat** lay in the middle of the war-zone. This refugee camp was in DRC.*

Refugees

Between 1990 and 1994, around a million Rwandan refugees fled to camps at the edge of the Virungas. It is estimated that while in the area, these refugees cut down around 36 million trees for firewood. Soldiers planted thousands of land-mines in the forest, endangering gorillas and researchers alike.

The consequences of war

The conflict has died down in recent years, but fighting still breaks out here and there. Nonetheless, Karisoke was reopened in 1999 and the researchers were able to resume their studies. The gorilla tourism industry will take longer to recover. In 1999, eight tourists were killed in Uganda, after they were abducted by Rwandan rebels. The warden (guard) of the Bwindi National Park was killed trying to protect the tourists, as were three of his rangers. More recently, three tourists were abducted by members of the same rebel group, and they have not been heard of since.

The situation in Rwanda has had very serious consequences for the local people, and for the gorillas. The pressure on the governments to make the land available to people for farming has increased even more. As long as the area remains so unstable, continuing to protect the animals and the forest is a huge challenge, and trying to develop gorilla tourism is just as problematic.

Conservation efforts

Although the mountain gorilla has been officially protected for nearly a hundred years, it is still a severely **endangered** animal. Its small population, limited **habitat** and slow **breeding** rate means it will be vulnerable to **extinction** for many years. The continued problems of habitat-loss, hunting, **poaching** and human conflict could still spell the end for the mountain gorilla.

Almost all the world's mountain gorillas live in the four official **national parks**. These areas are carefully guarded to try to keep the gorillas safe, and to keep people from cutting down the trees or grazing their **livestock** in the park. The job of being a park guard is difficult and dangerous. The guards require a lot of training, and they expect a good rate of pay. They are on the 'front line' of gorilla **conservation**.

Ongoing research into the lives of mountain gorillas is important for conservation.

Legal protection

The mountain gorilla has strict legal protection. It is listed in Appendix 1 by CITES (pronounced 'sightease'), the Convention on International Trade in Endangered Species of Wild Fauna and Flora. This is an international agreement by 161 nations to control and regulate trade in **endangered** wildlife. Nations can impose harsh penalties on people found guilty of poaching Appendix 1 animals. Hopefully this will deter poachers, but the more difficult it is to get hold of mountain gorilla body parts, the more collectors are willing to pay for them, so some poachers will still take the risk.

Justice

On 30 January 2003, three poachers were imprisoned for four years and fined about £2000 for killing gorillas in Rwanda. In May 2002, they had killed an adult female gorilla in order to steal her baby, and another adult female who had tried to protect the baby. The baby gorilla was rescued, and The Dian Fossey Gorilla Fund is attempting to return it to the wild.

Raising money is essential for gorilla research and protection. Model Rachel Hunter is seen here at a Born Free Foundation fundraising party in 2002.

Research and fundraising

Research helps scientists decide how best to protect the gorillas and the forest. The Mountain Gorilla Geomatics Project began in 1992, and concentrates on surveying the gorillas' movements and activities within the forest. The results of these surveys are analysed alongside maps of the forest's vegetation types, to work out how best to manage the habitat for the benefit of gorillas.

Research and guard patrols are expensive, so fundraising is important. The Dian Fossey Gorilla Fund is one of several organizations active in raising money for the conservation programme. Other wildlife **charities** make contributions. As well as directly funding conservation, the money is used to support the local community. This is an important part of gorilla conservation, because if local people are thriving they will not be a threat to the gorillas. Money can buy schoolbooks for children, pay for water cisterns to be installed and create credit funds to support the farmers living next to the forest.

When closely related animals breed together, their offspring are more likely to have health problems.

Thanks to the dedicated work of **conservationists**, the mountain gorilla population has increased in the last fifteen years. However, there are still well under a thousand mountain gorillas living today. They reproduce at a very slow rate, and only half of all babies survive to **breeding** age. Therefore, it will take a long time for mountain gorilla numbers to increase further.

The shrinking forest

Another problem that could keep gorilla numbers down is a shortage of suitable **habitat**. The forest they live in is completely surrounded by farmland, and it has become smaller and smaller over the years. There is room in the forest for more gorillas than there are at the moment, but it is very unlikely that mountain gorillas will ever live anywhere other than in the Virungas. It may be possible to increase the size of the forest by planting new trees, but it will take hundreds of years for them to grow big enough to form suitable habitat for the gorillas.

Captive breeding

Many **endangered** animals have been saved from **extinction** through captive breeding. Wild animals are caught and bred in captivity, where the babies can be completely protected from all danger. When they are old enough, the babies are released into the wild. This works well for some animals, but not for gorillas. Many of a gorilla's survival skills are learned rather than **instinctive**. If it grows up away from its natural habitat, it will not know how to find food and avoid danger.

Genetic problems

Yet another problem the mountain gorillas could face is one that can affect any very small animal population. In small, isolated populations, the animals often have very similar **genes** to each other, because no new animals ever arrive to breed with the rest and add new genes to the **gene pool**. If a disease spreads through the group and all gorillas share a low resistance to it, they might all die. Some scientists think that gorillas from the Virungas should be moved to Bwindi, or vice versa, so that the gene pool is enlarged, giving some group members better disease resistance.

A special animal

The mountain gorilla was probably already quite a rare animal before human activity put it in real danger. Today, it is very much rarer, but it is also one of the world's best-known and most familiar animals. Its magnificent appearance, impressive size and startling similarity to humans make it one of the most fascinating animals in the world. While this is the reason that **poachers** are so determined to hunt it, it is also why so many people are prepared to spend a great deal of time and money protecting it.

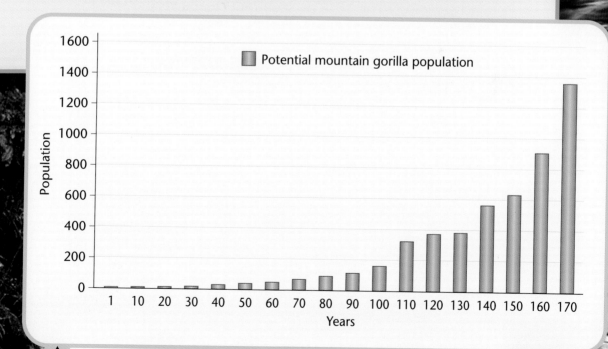

In theory, this is the rate at which mountain gorilla numbers would increase if there was no human interference.

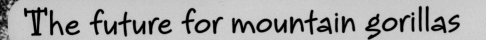

The future for mountain gorillas

It is hard to imagine a time in the future when mountain gorillas and their **habitat** will not need careful protection. **Poachers** are determined to hunt them, and their small habitat is constantly threatened with destruction. Political problems in the countries they live in could easily plunge the whole **conservation** operation into chaos again. However, there are many dedicated people, both local and from abroad, who are willing to work tirelessly to keep the gorillas away from the brink of **extinction**.

Mountain gorillas, the gentle giants of the wild **cloud-forest**, are one of the real treasures of the natural world.

Reasons to be hopeful

Mountain gorilla numbers are continuing slowly to increase. By sheer good luck, the direct impact of the war on their numbers was not too serious, and the **national parks** are now as well protected as they were before war broke out. The gorilla tourism industry is slowly recovering from the effect of the war, and the Rwandan government is working hard to build and maintain political stability and to attract more tourists. These efforts are bringing in more money, all of which is good for Rwanda and good for the gorillas.

Keeping up the good work

The ongoing work of researchers at Karisoke and other camps is also vital to help protect the gorillas. There is still a great deal to learn about gorilla behaviour and lifestyle. The effect of tourism on the gorillas is one important area for future research.

Returning to the wild

Often it is difficult to reunite rescued gorilla babies with their groups. In 1991, attempts were made to return a rescued two-and-a-half-year-old to her group. Unfortunately, the group rejected her and she had to be recaptured. A young female called Mvuyekure was rescued from poachers in October 2002. She was to be released in January 2003, but sadly she died before the attempt could be made. Despite many disappointments, researchers will continue to try to return any rescued young gorillas to their groups. With so few mountain gorillas left in the world, every single animal needs to have the best possible chance of living and **breeding** in the wild.

If the mountain gorilla is to survive, the forest must be protected from further destruction and the gorillas themselves must be protected from poachers. The best way to do this is to make sure that gorilla conservation goes hand-in-hand with supporting the local people.

How can you help?

Many wildlife **charities** collect donations to help with mountain gorilla **conservation**. The Dian Fossey Gorilla Fund is probably the most active. One of their popular schemes is 'Adopt a Gorilla'. For a donation of between £24 and £240 you receive an adoption certificate, a photograph of 'your' gorilla or gorillas and a t-shirt. This makes an unusual gift and is a fun way to help gorillas.

There are lots of ways you can raise money for gorilla charities, such as sponsored activities or a school jumble sale. Maybe you could sponsor your teacher to dress in a gorilla costume for a day!

Join in and speak up

Another way to support gorilla conservation, while learning more about them, is to become a member of a wildlife charity. For a small annual fee you will usually get regular magazines or newsletters telling you about the charity's work. The charity may organize events you can attend. It may also help you to make a difference, such as by telling you how to write to your Member of Parliament. Your MP has a duty to listen to your concerns, as well as the power to speak up about important issues in the House of Commons. Wealthy countries can do a great deal to help poorer countries with their conservation concerns.

Digit, the gorilla whose death led Dian Fossey to form the first mountain gorilla fundraising organization.

Support Africa and the forests

Gorilla tourism is an important source of money for conservation, as well as a magical experience. For the holiday of a lifetime, a gorilla-watching trek is hard to beat, and the money it raises for the country you visit benefits the gorillas too. If your family is going to consider a holiday like this, make sure that the tour company is responsible, and does not take too many tourists at a time to see the gorillas.

Encourage your family to check whenever they buy household objects made of wood that the wood has come from a **sustainable** source. Excessive **logging** has devastated many of the world's **rainforests**, putting all forest animals at risk of **extinction**.

Get muddy!

Learn more about the work of the gorilla conservationists, and perhaps even try some conservation work yourself. Working in conservation can be very tough, but it is extremely rewarding. There will always be a need for workers to monitor and study **endangered** animals. If you are interested in practical conservation work, you could join a local wildlife group and get involved in projects like pond digging, tree planting and counting wild animals. Developing skills like these is excellent preparation if one day you decide you would like to work with gorillas or other endangered animals.

Writing letters is a way of bringing the mountain gorilla's plight to the attention of those who can make a difference.

Glossary

aggression showing willingness to attack another animal

agriculture using land to grow crops or to graze domestic animals

alpha male dominant male gorilla in a group

apes types of primates with long arms and no tails

breed produce babies

canine long, pointed tooth or fang

charity non-profit-making organization set up to help others

cloud-forest montane forest, which is so high above sea-level that it is in the clouds

conservation working to protect wild animals and their habitats from destructive forces. A conservationist is someone who works in conservation.

development change aimed to improve land or habitat. Developers are the people who carry this out.

display activity performed by an animal that has a particular message (e.g. chest beating in gorillas signals aggression)

DRC Democratic Republic of the Congo, a country in central Africa. It was formally known as Zaire.

ecotourism kind of tourism that aims to benefit habitats, wildlife and local people

endangered when a plant or animal is in danger of dying out

equator imaginary line around the middle of the world, dividing it into northern and southern halves

extinction when a species or subspecies has died out and no longer exists

forage   to search for food

gene pool   all the genes of a group of animals, which are in contact with each other and breed together. A closely related group of animals have many of the same genes, so their gene pool is smaller.

genes   genes in living cells control how an organism looks and how it will survive, grow and change through its life

genetic testing   looking at an animal's genes in the laboratory, to see how closely related it is to other animals

great apes   five large apes: chimpanzees, bonobos, orang-utans, humans and gorillas

habitat   place in the natural world where a particular organism lives

habituate   to get a wild animal accustomed to human presence, so that it will behave normally even when humans are near by

harem   group of female animals who are all the partners of one male

herbivore   animal that eats plants

immunity   animal or person with an immunity to an infectious disease will not catch that disease from any other animal or person

infectious disease   disease that one animal can catch from another

instinctive   describes a behaviour that an animal 'knows' how to do without having to learn it

invertebrate   animal without a backbone

juvenile   young animal

livestock   animals kept for meat or milk, or to be sold

logging   cutting down (felling) trees. Loggers are the people who carry this out.

mammal warm-blooded animal with hair that can feed its young with milk from its body

montane environment that is found on the slopes of mountains

national park area of natural beauty protected by law

parasite tiny animal that lives on or inside another animal's body. Large numbers of parasites can cause illness.

poaching catching or killing an animal illegally

predator animal that hunts and eats other animals

primates group of mammals including lemurs, bushbabies, monkeys and apes. Most are tree-climbing plant-eaters that live in forests.

rainforest ancient, mature forest found close to the equator, which has very heavy rainfall

silverback fully adult male gorilla

snare trap to catch a wild animal

species type of animal that cannot breed successfully with any other type

subspecies distinct type that can breed with other subspecies within a species

sustainable way of farming or logging that can be carried out continuously without permanently harming or altering the land it uses

taboo activity that people avoid, because they believe it is wrong, unhealthy or will bring bad luck

territory particular area an animal claims as its own and defends from others

weaned when an animal no longer takes milk from its mother

Useful contacts and further reading

Conservation groups and websites

The Dian Fossey Gorilla Fund
www.dianfossey.org
The Dian Fossey Gorilla Fund
110 Gloucester Avenue
London NW1 8HX UK

The Mountain Gorilla Geomatics project
www.informatics.org/gorilla/gorilla.html

WWF
www.panda.org

National Geographic magazine
www.nationalgeographic.com/kids/creature_feature/0007/gorillas.html
This is an interesting feature all about mountain gorillas.

Books

Dian Fossey (Groundbreakers), Richard and Sarah Wood
(Heinemann Library, 2002)

Earth Files: Forests, Anita Ganeri (Heinemann Library, 2002)

Gorilla: Struggle for Survival in the Virungas, Michael Nicholls
(Aperture, 1992)

Gorillas in the Mist, Dian Fossey (Penguin, 1988)

Mountain Gorilla: Ecology and Behaviour, George Schaller (University of
Chicago Press, 1963)

What's at issue? War and Conflict, Sean Connolly
(Heinemann Library, 2001)

Year of the Gorilla, George Schaller (University of Chicago Press, 1966)

Index

Titles in the *Animals Under Threat* series include:

Hardback   0 431 18892 0

Hardback   0 431 18888 2

Hardback   0 431 18889 0

Hardback   0 431 18893 9

Hardback   0 431 18890 4

Hardback   0 431 18891 2

Find out about the other titles in this series on our website www.heinemann.co.uk/library